Attracting Your Godly Spouse:
A Study Guide for Finding
Lasting Love

By

Jeremy Lopez

Attracting Your Godly Spouse: A Study Guide
for Finding Lasting Love
By Dr. Jeremy Lopez
Copyright © 2018

Published by Identity Network
P.O. box 383213
Birmingham, AL 35238

www.IdentityNetwork.net

ENDORSEMENTS

"You are put on this earth with incredible potential and a divine destiny. This powerful, practical man shows you how to tap into powers you didn't even know you had." – Brian Tracy – Author, The Power of Self Confidence

"I found myself savoring the concepts of the Law of Attraction merging with the Law of Creativity until slowly the beautiful truths seeped deeper into my thirsty soul. I am called to be a Creator! My friend, Dr. Jeremy Lopez, has a way of reminding us of our eternal 'I-Am-ness' while putting the tools in our hands to unlock our endless creative potential with the Divine mind. As a musical composer, I'm excited to explore, with greater understanding, the infinite realm of possibilities as I place fingers on my piano and whisper, 'Let there be!'" – Dony McGuire, Grammy Award winning artist and musical composer

"Jeremy dives deep into the power of consciousness and shows us that we can create a world where the champion within us can shine and how we can manifest our desires to live a life of fulfillment. A must read!" – Greg S. Reid – Forbes and Inc. top rated Keynote Speaker

"I have been privileged to know Jeremy Lopez for many years, as well as sharing the platform with him at a number of conferences. Through this time,

I have found him as a man of integrity, commitment, wisdom, and one of the most networked people I have met. Jeremy is an entrepreneur and a leader of leaders. He has amazing insights into leadership competencies and values. He has a passion to ignite this latent potential within individuals and organizations and provide ongoing development and coaching to bring about competitive advantage and success. I would recommend him as a speaker, coach, mentor, and consultant." – Chris Gaborit – Learning Leader, Training & Outsourcing Expert, Entrepreneur

CONTENTS

INTRODUCTION

Chances are you're reading this study guide because you're also reading my newest, best-selling book *Attracting Your Godly Spouse* and now find yourself at a point in your life where you're tired of the loneliness and isolation and are ready to begin your search for true and lasting love. I want to say, right here at the offset, I applaud your efforts and am so thrilled that you've made the decision to reclaim control of your life and your relationships. Life is filled with many extraordinary and wonderful relationships – connections with people. I've said for years that, in the end of things, life will not be measured only by the successes and the moments that we've created but, much more so, by the people we've enjoyed those moments with. Relationships matter, both here and in the Kingdom of Heaven. Relationships are eternal and they're important. As you'll see, as you read my book

Attracting Your Godly Spouse, it's important that you and I begin to view all of our relationships and all of our connections in a much more spiritual way – through spiritual eyes. In order to begin to do this, though, a few things have to change within our minds. Old mindsets must first be stripped away and we must be confronted with the reality that every connection we make and every relationship we've enjoyed, are currently enjoying, or ever will enjoy we've attracted in our own lives in some way, based entirely upon our thoughts and our own mindsets.

If you've followed my work for any amount of time, then you know full well that I so often speak on the topic on the universal Law of Attraction. This power of attraction is crucial to literally each and every element of daily life – particularly in our relationships. As we go throughout life, we encounter many wonderful and interesting people. Some of these relationship connections are enjoyed much, much more than the others. Some are platonic, while others are of a more romantic nature.

I sense you're reading this book because you now find yourself ready to begin the search to find real and lasting love and to finally attract into your life the person of your very own dreams and desires. As you'll see when reading my book, in order to do this, you're going to have to first learn to become much, much more attractive than you've been. Now, let me say here at the start that when I'm referring to you becoming much more attractive, I'm in no way referring to your physical, outward appearance. I'm referring, instead, to the all-important, all-powerful "makeover" of the mind. If you're truly ready to find real and lasting love and romance and are desperate to experience that spark of chemistry, you're going to have to first begin to change the way that you view love and relationships. As with all things in life, you have a role to play.

For decades, I've had the privilege and honor of connecting with individuals, just like you, and sharing with them powerful principles and techniques and strategies that, when implemented, lead to greater success, greater abundance, and a much, much more abundant life. Over the years, I've counseled and coached so many individuals in matters of business and in all matters of life. One question that I'm asked, perhaps more than all others, is, "Jeremy, when will I finally meet the right person?" I can't even tell you how often I'm asked this most burning, pressing question. You see, you and I, by divine design, were created to experience the joys of relationship and, yes, we were created by a very loving Creator to crave romance and chemistry. From the very beginning of it all, even in the garden paradise, there existed a love story between two people. Not only is it completely natural and healthy to want to find real and lasting love, but it's a very spiritual, very beautiful thing. Unfortunately, however, all too often, we succumb to our own inner fears and insecurities where love is concerned, and we stop short before ever finding the person of our dreams and desires. Other times, we often sabotage our own connections because of these same inner fears and insecurities. That's why, long before we ever even begin the search, it's vitally important that we first get to know ourselves and get in touch with our own dreams and desires. If you don't know who you are and what it is you truly want, how will you ever know when you've found it?

From the very beginning, by divine design, you and I were given dominion by GOD over all of creation. This law of dominion established by the Creator set a precedent for the universal Law of Attraction – the force that resides within our own will and within our very own thoughts. Did you know that everything – literally everything – exists within our lives based upon what we think? It's true! I share much, much more about the powerful principles of the Law of Attraction and the Law of Creation in my best-selling book *Creating with Your Thoughts*, and you can find this and many other powerful resources on techniques for harnessing the power of the mind by contacting the offices of Identity Network today; however, suffice it to say that even our very own relationships are fueled by our thoughts. Although it may seem to be a very bitter pill to swallow right now, the relationships in your life – or the apparent lack of relationships – is a result of your very own thoughts. If you're reading this book and find yourself seemingly plagued by the sense of loneliness and isolation and if it feels as though you'll never meet that special someone, it isn't because of how you look and it most certainly isn't because you aren't deserving of love; it's because of what you've thought. Yes, you read that correctly. You love life, just like all other matters of life, is a direct result of the way you see yourself. So, as we begin this powerful journey of attraction together, I want to ask you a very important question, my friend: "How do you see yourself?"

In order to raise your own creative, attractive power, you're going to have to, first, take a long hard look in the mirror and see the reflection of your very own mind. If you're truly ready to attract into your life the person of your very own dreams and desire and if you're truly ready to begin to experience the love and romance you were destined to enjoy, it's time to begin to reclaim your own attraction. This is the reason why this entire *Attracting your Godly Spouse* series was designed – to help you to harness your own attraction. The power begins, though, when you begin to change the way that you see yourself. If you see yourself as someone insecure and undeserving of love, how can you possibly expect someone else – another person – to actually take you seriously? It's hypocritical, really, to expect someone else to invest their time in you if you haven't first begun to invest in yourself. The universe doesn't work that way. Heaven doesn't work that way. Furthermore, quite simply put, we as humans aren't designed to operate in that way. Each and every morning, you are presenting an image to the world around you, based entirely upon what you think about yourself. This image contains power, because it's fueled by your very own thoughts and intention. You see, it's the intention which is truly the power behind the Law of Attraction, and if it's your intention to draw into your life the connection of your dreams, well it's time to stop dreaming and start moving!

I know right now you're probably thinking, "Jeremy, he could never love me the way I am." In twenty years of working with the Law of Attraction, I've heard it all before. "I'm too fat." "I'm too skinny." "I don't make enough money." "I'm not confident enough." At the end of the day, though, it's all the same excuse, really: "I'm too afraid." In case you haven't noticed, fear paralyzes us from moving forward and from beginning to reclaim the stories of our lives. Today, as you begin this book, Heaven is asking you a very simple question: "What do you truly want to find in your search for love?" The way in which you answer that question, my friend, will determine exactly what – and who – you begin to draw into your life. The power of attraction is so powerful, in fact, that it can often be quite scary. The universe and all of Heaven will give you exactly what and who you want, based entirely upon the way you see yourself. So, knowing this, isn't it time that you start to view yourself in a much, much different light? Today, as we begin this journey together, I want to encourage you to begin to recognize that you deserve the very best of what the universe has to offer you. You are worthy of love. You are deserving of romance. You deserve to experience and enjoy all that relationships have to offer. It's time that you begin to see yourself the way Heaven sees you, and this starts by looking in the mirror at your own mindset.

Nearly twenty years ago, when I began this work in prophetic coaching, I found myself bombarded with questions about love and romance. Beautiful, sincere people, just like you, wanted to know what the Spirit was saying to them about their love lives. The answer was usually quite simple: "Get out and start moving!" This truth often was a very difficult pill for many to swallow, though, because religion has always seemed to suggest that in order to find the person of your dreams, you have to sit idly by and wait on GOD. I'm sure you're quite familiar with this mindset and with the sense of overwhelming confusion it can cause. I so often hear, "Jeremy, I don't believe in dating. I have faith that GOD will send someone new into my singles' group at church." Well, it can absolutely happen. You could also win the lottery or be struck by lightning. I mean, anything's possible. Now, I don't say that to cause you to question your faith in any way. I say that to simply point out, aren't you tired of viewing your life in such an uncertain way, like some game of chance? Aren't you tired of sitting idly by and waiting for GOD to manifest some miracle in your life when, the entire time, all of Heaven is seeking to inspire you to get up, get out, and start to use your own creative, attractive power to write your own love story? If so, then this book series is for you, my friend!

It's time to get up, get out, and start moving. It's time to begin to experience the adventures and the connections of life in a much, much different way. It's time to reclaim the power in your life – the power that you've for so long unknowingly been giving away to other people. It's time to finally begin to discover who you truly are and what you're truly deserving of. It's time to attract into your life the love and romance you've been dreaming of. When I wrote *Attracting Your Godly Spouse*, I did so because I wanted to answer, once and for all, all of those questions that seem to come up when people begin to think of just exactly "how" to attract the love and romance they desire. In the book, I shared time-tested and proven prophetic strategies designed to inspire you to truly harness your own attractive power. In fact, as far as books dealing with the subject of love and relationships go, the book is the first of its kind. In it, I share powerful principles geared toward helping you to harness your own power and literally rev up the attractive power you're working with. I also released, as an accompanying workbook, *Attracting Your Godly Spouse: A Workbook in Attraction* as a literal 11 day intensive training guide to help you to harness your own power even more. If you haven't already done so, I would highly, highly recommend you get the book to complete your collection of the entire *Attracting Your Godly Spouse* series. All of these products and more can be obtained by contacting the offices of Identity Network.

I want you to use this study guide, as well as the specially designed workbook, in tandem with my best-selling book as a way to go even further and even deeper into your own attractive power. In fact, there are additional tips in the accompanying workbook which you will not find in this companion study guide so, again, I highly recommend you get your copy today! This study guide, *Attracting Your Godly Spouse*, will serve as a much-needed tool as you begin your work to help you in going even further in harnessing your own, true, attractive power. There's a special sort of magic that happens when we begin to yield to the voice of the inner Kingdom of Heaven and become more sensitive to the voice of the Holy Spirit and to our own intuition. As we surrender more and more, we begin to see that it has always been the will of GOD for us to enjoy and experience this vast, big, beautiful world and literally all of the many, many connections and relationships we encounter each day. My friend, you've never been as out of control as you've been feeling, I promise you. Each day, GOD has given you a choice to create your life experiences, based upon the power of the divine mind of the Godhead within you, inside the inner Kingdom of Heaven. The truth of the matter is that you've always been good enough. You've always been worthy enough. You've always been worthy and deserving of love. The issue, though, has always been that you've never really taken the time to truly see it. Our work together will begin to change that and propel you forward into a greater ability to harness your own attractive, creative power.

Far too often, as you'll see, we give our power away to other people. Rather than knowing who we are and what we want in relationships, we choose, rather, to base our lives upon he feelings, thoughts, desires, and wishes of other people. By doing this, we stifle our own voice of attractive power. Today, as we begin our journey together, I want to encourage you to stop seeing yourself as just an "extra" in someone else's life and begin, instead, to see yourself as the co-creator with GOD you've always been destined to be. It's time to reclaim your love life and begin to see who you truly are. In order to do this, though, some work will be required. In order to do this, you're going to have to start to actually learn to love yourself again. It may be difficult at first, and in the beginning, you may be thinking, "Jeremy, I don't really even like myself, let alone love myself." It's okay. Our work together will help. I want to make you a promise, my friend. Although there truly is no magic formula or any magical prophetic prayer that can be prayed to miraculously manifest someone in your life, I promise you that if you will commit to doing the work and commit to beginning to shift your perspective, you will attract into your life a new and lasting relationship within the next 90 days. I assure you of that. That is, if you do the work.

As you read the book, *Attracting Your Godly Spouse*, this study guide will serve as a companion for you, giving you even more insight as you progress through the book, chapter by chapter. You will need to have a copy of the book, as you use this companion study guide. And, each day, the workbook will be an even greater aid in helping you to begin to put into practice what you learn. This series – the very first of its kind – is designed by the Holy Spirit to help you finally begin to unlock the true power behind all of your relationships. When you begin to finally see that, although it may not always seem like it, you truly are the one in control, I promise you that you'll begin to view all of your relationships in a much, much different way. No longer will dating seem like such a draining, constant struggle. Instead, all of your connections will begin to see like other opportunities to enjoy your life. Are you ready? Are you ready to change your life and begin to write the love story of your dreams and desires? Are you ready to not only attract a relationship but, instead, attract the exact person of your dreams? Well, it's time to change your mind, and that begins today. A brand new you can begin today, if you're prepared to see who you truly are and what you truly deserve. Today is the day you awaken to the love story you've been dreaming about.

CHAPTER ONE

In Chapter One, entitled "Knowing your Vision," the emphasis of the teaching is on learning to recognize the importance of knowing exactly who you are and exactly what you desire. This chapter is incredibly important because it deals with setting your intention at the very beginning of your journey and creating a clear, inner vision within, which will serve as the basis of your search as you begin to start attracting more quality relationships. As you progress through the chapter you're shown a series of practical illustrations from real-life clients I've mentored throughout the years and are also given a few real-life scenarios about dating. The reason for this is because it's important to already begin to view yourself in real-life dating scenarios, even before ever meeting the person you desire. What will the conversation be like? What moments will you want to share, as you embark together upon those first moments of getting to know each other?

It's vitally important that you begin to already paint within your mind the image of what you want to accomplish and what you're wanting to experience. Self-awareness is crucial when speaking of the universal Law of Attraction. In order to be able to attract what or whom you're wanting into your life, you must first have within your mind a crystal clear image of who you are and what you deserve. A feeling of unworthiness will hinder your progress and will stifle your creative power. Often, because of religious tradition, individuals feel a sense of unworthiness – feeling as if they are undeserving of receiving the very best. Throughout the chapter, I continually stressed the importance of self-awareness when considering beginning the pursuit of finding lasting love. Can you think of key examples from your own life which, in times past, have hindered you from enjoying successful relationships or from making new connections? If so, were you hindered by what the other person may or may not have been thinking? Did you often find yourself putting on a façade or seemingly wearing a mask, in order to impress the other person? Whether you realized it at the time or not, you stifled your own confidence and your own creativity by not allowing your true and authentic self to shine through. This is a common mistake that we all have made at one time or another.

In a fascinating article in the October issue of *Psychology Today* entitled "Self-confidence versus self-esteem," Dr. Neel Burton writes, "People usually find it easier to build their self-confidence than their self-esteem, and, conflating one with the other, end up with a long list of abilities and achievements. Rather than facing up to their imperfections and failures, they hide them behind their certificates and prizes. But as anyone who has been to university knows, a long list of abilities and achievements is neither sufficient nor necessary for healthy self-esteem. While people keep on working on their list in the hope that it might one day be long enough, they try to fill the emptiness inside them with status, income, possessions, relationships, sex, and so on." I agree wholeheartedly. This *emptiness* which he describes is rooted in a lack of true self-awareness and an inability to know and to understand the true and authentic self. Looking back, how many times have you in times past sought to put on a façade to impress others by hiding behind your accomplishments or your accolades or how often have you used your success as a sort of wall to hide behind? We've all been guilty of this at one time or another. By learning to become more self-aware – secure in the knowledge of who you are – you will, in turn, begin to recognize that the story of your life and the many, many varying traits and characteristics that you have to offer serve to paint a picture of a whole and complete person. You will then begin to see and to recognize that you have always been complete within yourself the entire time and that there is truly no need to look to others or even to your own accomplishments for the sense of validation.

Throughout the chapter, you've found that in life you aren't merely some "extra" who has been cast in other people's films but are, rather, your own leading star in the film of your own life. This shift of perspective is necessary to not only move from the place of insecurity to the place of confidence but also is vital to boost your own sense of self-confidence and self-esteem. You are completely unique because of the story of your life and because of your many desires, dreams, and interests, not in spite of them. Your differences are not liabilities but are, rather, part of the makeup of your own unique individuality. Can you, in your own life, think of times in which you felt insecure because of your dreams and desires, feeling as though others might not view you favorably if they were to know the real you? Have you, in times past, built a wall through your communication and evaded and avoided certain questions about yourself, solely for the reason that you felt the other person might judge you harshly or unfavorably if they knew the full truth? If so, you were unknowingly being an "extra," believing yourself to be simply a background character in someone else's film – you were unknowingly failing to assume the leading role within our very own life.

In my best-selling book *Creating with Your Thoughts*, I discussed how, as visual beings, you and I are given, by divine design, the ability to see our thoughts. In a sense, you and I have been given front row seats to the "movie" of our lives and have been given the ability to actually view our thoughts. As each thought passes, because of the power of creation, you and I are constantly being asked, "Do you want to create this?" Unknowingly, at times, because of our own fears and our own inability to accept ourselves and the story of our lives in its entirety, we are without realizing it creating situations which repel others rather than attract them to us. The other people notice the evasion and our avoidance in answering certain things. Though you don't have to volunteer information, if the reason for your lack of communication is fear, then you are unknowingly creating a barrier which is hindering the power of your own attraction – all because you have not fully owned who it is that you truly are.

I want you to begin to see yourself clearly not only as your own unique and timeless individual but also as a vessel of the Kingdom of Heaven possessing all of the unique qualities and characteristics which make you so very special. It's time to remove the mask. The word "person" is actually derived from the Latin "persona," which means "mask." In order to begin to fully harness your own creative and attractive power in your relationships, you're going to have to learn to remove the mask, as frightening as it might be. In order to do this, a little self-acceptance will be required of you. Until you can begin to see yourself the way Heaven sees you, you will never be able to truly see yourself the way other people see you. This is what I mean by self-awareness – knowing who you are and knowing the role you play. Begin to let the role you play be the leading role of your own life and not simply some "extra" or some "stand-in" in the film of someone else's life. Begin to own your own desires and your own interests. If you enjoy a certain band and a certain type of music, don't be afraid to own it. If you enjoy a certain food, never be afraid to say so. If you're feeling as though the other person might not accept your wishes, wants, and desires, then it's alright to walk away. Remember, you have options and there's a great, big world out there. However, for now, it's time to begin to remove the mask. How can you ever truly expect another person to truly accept you for who you are when you haven't even fully accepted yourself or given them the opportunity to get to know the real you?

CHAPTER TWO

In Chapter Two, entitled, "Attraction 101," I share powerful spiritual principles behind the "feeling" of attraction. For far too long, you've viewed romantic attraction and physical chemistry solely from the perspective of the physical, rather than being sensitive to the inner dynamic of the energy in play. Throughout the chapter, I share practical examples of how the chemistry is felt as two people are drawn to each other. In the instant of the preliminary feeling, it can seem as though the attraction is based solely on the physical; however, by taking a deeper look, we find that the visual perception of the outward, physical appearance is merely an extra added bonus and that the true source of the chemistry is stemming from the energetic bond being formed. Remember, everything is energy – including the sense of chemistry and attraction we feel when making initial connections for relationships. Although, at first glance, it might seem as though attraction is based purely upon the visual response to the outward appearance, a variety of other dynamics are also in play, internally. As I shared within my book *Creating with Your Thoughts*, by divine design you and I are visual beings, created by GOD with the divine ability to actually see our own thoughts as a movie upon the screen of the mind's eye. Well, there's a very real scientific reason for this, and it has literally everything to do with the brain and the makeup of the brain.

In a February 2017 article by Katherine Wu entitled "Love Actually: The Science Behind Lust, Attraction, and Companionship," shared by the Harvard University Graduate School of Arts and Sciences, Wu states, "Meanwhile, attraction seems to be a distinct, though closely related, phenomenon. While we can certainly lust for someone we are attracted to, and vice versa, one can happen without the other. Attraction involves the brain pathways that control "reward" behavior, which partly explains why the first few weeks or months of a relationship can be so exhilarating and even all-consuming. Dopamine, produced by the hypothalamus, is a particularly well-publicized player in the brain's reward pathway – it's released when we do things that feel good to us. In this case, these things include spending time with loved ones and having sex. High levels of dopamine and a related hormone, norepinephrine, are released during attraction. These chemicals make us giddy, energetic, and euphoric, even leading to decreased appetite and insomnia – which means you actually can be so "in love" that you can't eat and can't sleep. In fact, norepinephrine, also known as noradrenalin, may sound familiar because it plays a large role in the fight or flight response, which kicks into high gear when we're stressed and keeps us alert. Brain scans of people in love have actually shown that the primary "reward" centers of the brain, including the and the caudate nucleus, fire like crazy when people are shown a photo of someone they are intensely attracted to, compared to when they are shown someone they feel neutral towards (like an old high school acquaintance). Finally, attraction seems to lead to a reduction in serotonin, a hormone that's known to be involved in appetite and mood. Interestingly, people who suffer from obsessive-compulsive disorder also have low levels of serotonin, leading scientists to speculate that this is what underlies the overpowering infatuation that characterizes the beginning stages of love."

As you can see, the functioning of the brain plays a very integral role in the way that we interpret the many varying feelings associated with chemistry, lust, attraction, and even the feeling of love, and these inner, internal workings are paramount to seeing that attraction isn't just purely physical – it's in many ways biological and emotional; therefore it's spiritual. Although you and I are created by the divine design of a very loving and artful Creator to be visual beings, so often we can become so inundated by the physical that we often unknowingly neglect the emotions at work with each passing sight. As a result, we very rarely ever take the time to be thoughtful and truly present in our emotions. We're led by sight, rather than by the inner voice which speaks in tandem with our emotions. Because of this, we so often view all of our connections in very shallow, extremely superficial ways. We've all done this at times, often without ever even knowing it. Can you think of moments in which, at first glance, you felt the instantaneous, almost overwhelming attraction to someone to the point where you literally felt that you'd lose control? Did you feel the physiological and biological response? The cold, sweaty palms and the elevated heartbeat? This outward, physical response is the very real result of a very divine, internal process within the brain. By learning to become much more sensitive to the emotions behind the feelings, we can begin to become much more thoughtful in the way that we view chemistry and attraction. Both chemistry and attraction are divine and very heavenly aspects of romantic relationships, and by becoming more sensitive to the inner feeling, at the moment it's felt, we can begin to bring a newfound sense of thoughtfulness and self-awareness to the way in which we pursue romantic connections.

In the chapter, I shared a powerful illustration of "boy meets girl" that, in many ways, can depict the internal process of the way in which we can at times seemingly also overanalyze the feeling of chemistry and attraction. When boy meets girl – or when anyone meets anyone else, for that matter – if there is a moment of attraction and an initial speak of chemistry, it can at times seem quite frightening in the beginning. Let's face it; it can feel a little overwhelming. Often, in the midst of this initial, overwhelming feeling, there are also the flashes of our own programmed conditioning, as we ask a series of questions, all in an instant. "Should I want this?" "Is this right?" "What exactly am I feeling?" "How do I proceed?" With all of these questions, comes an even more overwhelming need to gain a sense of clarity and, in the midst of overwhelming emotion, the clarity can, at times, seem nonexistent. The reason that I chose to include within the book the chapter entitled "Attraction 101" is because I want you to see – to truly understand – that, yes, there is a very real sense of spirituality at work even within the most unexpected and most random moments of chemistry. You and I are given a choice, upon feeling it, of how we wish to proceed, and we have been given control over our feelings.

Contrary to popular belief, it actually is possible to take a step back, even in those instantaneous moments of chemistry, and ask, "Why am I feeling this?" In other words, it's alright and it's actually very healthy to question our own social, societal, and even religious programming. Doing this will, in turn help to give us a sense of clarity of what and even who we truly want. Once we begin to develop the ability – the sensitivity – to look beyond the inner chatter and the inner noise of the emotions, we can become even more thoughtful of how to proceed and move forward when we feel the overwhelming and instantaneous feelings of magnetism so associated with our search for lasting love. Another element we must consider is also the role intuition plays. Being that everything truly is energy, attraction, to some degree is a signal of openness. Now, I'm not suggesting that each and every person you feel attracted to feels the exact same way about you; however what I am saying is that the feeling of attraction exists for a reason. You aren't feeling the attraction simply because GOD wants to tease you or play tricks with your feelings. This is why intuition and sensitivity to the voice of the Holy Spirit is so incredibly important. By learning to become sensitive to the inner voice of the Holy Spirit – the voice of the Kingdom of Heaven within – you and I begin to become more thoughtful to not only the "why" and the "how" regarding chemistry, but we can also become more aware of the "what's next?"

CHAPTER THREE

In Chapter Three, entitled "Heavenly Love," I share several principles which deal with the way in which we actually view the idea of "love." Now that we've established the role that attraction and chemistry play in making connections and forming romantic relationships, it's time to take an even deeper look into the topic of love itself. Whether you realize it, consciously, or not, the way in which you define love will be the basis by which all of your romantic connections will be enacted. Remember that everything stems from the intention that we set and that it's through our true intention that the universe and all of Heaven and earth respond to us through the universal, heavenly power of the Law of Attraction. In other words, if you're truly going to attract love, it's vital that you have a proper understanding of what you truly mean when you say "love." Only you can define this in your own way; however, in the chapter entitled

"Heavenly Love," I wanted to share with you a bit of a new and fresh perspective on the matter – a new perspective to consider.

It simply cannot be understated just how much of an influential role religion and religious tradition has played and continues to play in helping to craft our view of "love," even when we don't fully realize it. I'm in no way saying this to imply that this is either a "good" or a "bad" thing; however, what I am saying is that whether you realize it or not you've been programmed to believe a certain thing and to hold to a particular worldview, whether you realize it or not. If you have yet to get your copies of my best-selling books *Creating with Your Thoughts* and *The Universe is at Your Command*, I would strongly encourage you to do so by contacting the offices of Identity Network, because in those two books I share very insightful, yet practical truth about how in order to truly harness the power of the universal and heavenly Law of Attraction we must, first, look beyond our preconceived notions and our own programming and indoctrination in order to truly get in touch with what I call "authentic desire." Finding authentic desire is not an easy process, to be quite honest; however, if you are ever going to truly master the art of creating the life you want by harnessing the power of your own thoughts, you're going to have to, first, become aware of what it is that you truly want.

For far, far too long you and I have been conditioned – programmed – to view desire in such a negative way. This programming has inadvertently caused us to be "double-minded" in literally all of our pursuits – including our search for love and romance. Allow me to explain further. When you have a desire in your heart and an inner vision established within your mind, if you continually question it or, even worse, continue to question your right to have it, you are, as the Book of James says, "Double minded." The Book of James goes on to make the very bold declaration that double-minded people shouldn't even expect to receive anything from GOD at all! That's a rather bold statement, I know, but it's true! I know you're probably thinking, "Jeremy, what does that truly mean?" The passage from the Book of James regarding "double-mindedness," perhaps more than all other verses throughout the entirety of the scriptures details the importance of establishing a concrete vision and understanding your true and authentic desire. In other words, once you come to know what it truly is that you want and desire and once you've established the decree within your mind, hold fast to the profession of faith.

Perhaps the greatest, most simple, yet transcendent definition of "love" is, quite literally GOD. In two very real and very emphatic declarations throughout the scriptures, GOD is literally defined in two ways: as "love" and as "Spirit." Knowing this, perhaps you now have a better understanding of why I felt the need and the inspiration to write the book *Attracting Your Godly Spouse*, to share the powerful truth that the search for love and romance is actually quite spiritual and a process to be enjoyed. The scriptures make these two bold declarations regarding the "definition" of GOD in this way: "He that loveth not knoweth not God; for God is love." (1 John 4:8 KJV) "God is a Spirit: and they that worship him must worship him in spirit and in truth." (John 4:24 KJV) Now knowing this, can you now see the great importance of viewing the idea of even romantic love in a more spiritual way? Part of the reason I chose to include the chapter "Heavenly Love" within the book is because I truly want you to stop condemning yourself. I want you to stop blaming yourself for wanting what it is - or even who it is – that you want and find yourself magnetically drawn to. Stop condemning the very desires that are coming from the Spirit of GOD within you!

Can you see how, perhaps, in your own life there have moments when you've overanalyzed and, as a result, have talked yourself out of moving forward with certain desires, all because you felt a sense of condemnation in wanting it? Can you think of moments in your life when, because of your own fear of wanting you ended your search and ended your pursuit of obtainment? My friend, there is no condemnation to those who believe. Part of the reason why it's so very important to begin to view love and, yes, even the pursuit of love in a more heavenly and divine way – through spiritual eyes – is, quite simply, because GOD is "love" and GOD is "Spirit." The two are forever linked and eternally intertwined.

CHAPTER FOUR

In Chapter Four, entitled "The Search," I shared the importance of actually beginning to put action and movement to your faith by starting to get up, get out, and actually begin the search for the relationship of your dreams and desires. Fans of music will be familiar with the hit Motown song by Smokey Robinson and the Miracles, "Shop Around." In the hit song, the lyrics serve as a reminder that, when considering "dating," you have lots of options out there. The reason I wanted to include the chapter "The Search" is because many times, when speaking of dating and when thinking of the moments where we actually form the connections which could quite possibly lead to very real and lasting relationships, we often forget that there are plenty of options available, although, at times, it may not seem that way. In the chapter, I shared the importance of actually beginning to put movement and action to your faith and to your desires and your intention.

When we speak of the subject of the heavenly power of the Law of Attraction, it isn't enough to simply sit idly by on the sidelines and have an intention. Intention, alone, is nothing more than daydreaming. Faith and true intention requires action. In fact, perhaps the best way to describe the true meaning of intention is in this way: "Intention is a vision so strong that is causes you to act." For more than twenty years, I've taught the power of intention and that, by harnessing our thoughts and our intentions, we are prophetically making a declaration to the universe and to all of Heaven and earth, saying, "This is my desire!" However, the intention alone isn't enough to bring about your true and authentic desire. Movement and a step of faith are also required. Now, I know that when we speak of actually getting up, getting out, and starting to move around in the dating world, the feelings associated with such talk can seem quite frightening. It's okay. I understand. It's one thing to have within our minds and within our hearts a concept of what romance should look like or even feel like, but it can feel like another matter entirely when the time comes to finally need to put action behind our faith. Stepping out can seem like the frightening and the overwhelming part; however, it's necessary.

According to the scriptures, faith without works is meaningless. In other words, the faith – the intention, alone – is nothing without the added movement. I've said for years in my teachings regarding the universal Law of Attraction and within my many, many teachings regarding the power of the prophetic voice that faith requires movement. We see this principle being enacted all throughout the entirety of the scriptures. When it was the lame being asked to stand up, the blind being asked to wash their eyes, the need for the stone to be rolled away in order for the dead to be raised, all faith required action – movement – in some way. I like to think of movement as our agreement with Heaven that says, "I'm truly ready for this." This is perhaps never any more true than when we speak of the need to put movement behind our thoughts and intentions regarding the search for true and lasting love and when attempting to find the person of our dreams and desires. This is the reason I chose to entitle the chapter "The Search."

The scriptures make it plain that those who "find" a partner find a good thing! In order to "find," though, one must search. This implies action. You aren't going to be able to simply sit idly by on the sidelines of life, waiting and hoping that one day, miraculously, GOD will drop someone into your lap. Furthermore, you aren't going to be able to just sit back and hope that one day a single, attractive, eligible man will just so happen to stroll into your singles' group at church. The universe demands action. The Kingdom of Heaven recognizes faith but responds and begins to move when a step is taken. Now, I know that, for you, perhaps the beginning of the "search" has seemed like the most frightening part. In truth, it's that way for all of us. It's one thing to visualize and to even be able to believe that a successful relationships exists; however, actually getting up and getting moving can be a little daunting, I'll admit. It's okay. As you think of this in your own life, how would you describe the feelings associated with your search for relationships and the feelings associated with dating? All too often I hear the feeling described in this way: "Jeremy, it just all seems so exhausting." I can understand that. Far, far too often we've viewed the process of dating and, well, the process of "shopping around" in such an exhausting way and, as a result we've added so much unnecessary stress and burden to the process. My friend, it doesn't have to be that way. That's the purpose of this book series – to help you to be able to become much more strategic in your decisions regarding the pursuit of relationships.

I want you to begin to become much, much more strategic in your decision making when considering moving forward in a relationship. Without strategic decision making, the search for love is left simply to chance, and it doesn't have to be this way. In fact, there's a better way. When you begin to, first, get in touch with yourself and realize who you truly are and what you are truly deserving of, then you will be able to take control of your love life and begin to reclaim your own attractive, creative power. The entire time you've been sitting idly by waiting for GOD to bring into your life the person of your dreams and desires, Heaven has been waiting on you! The time to act is now – today – and there's never any time like the present. This is your NOW moment! Remember that all change begins, first, with a decision to act. I hope and pray that by reading the book not only have you begun to view all of your relationships from a much different, more heavenly perspective but that you've also become inspired to recognize that there's a great, big world out there just waiting to be enjoyed and explored. From the very beginning, when the original love story first began in the garden paradise, the Creator gave mankind the mission to have dominion over the earth. In a sense, the Creator was saying to the crowning jewel of His

Creation, "Enjoy!" Part of learning to harness your own attractive power comes from taking bold, strategic moves – moves that cause you to have to move outside of your comfort zone and your areas of familiarity.

I was once speaking to a young woman – a real life client whose testimony I included in the book – and she was facing the fear and the crippling paralysis that so often comes when we begin to think of beginning the search for lasting love. She said to me, "Jeremy, I'm waiting on GOD, but I know that I'm not getting any younger." I admired her faith and her passion for the LORD. I asked, "Are you getting out and meeting new people?" She replied, simply, "No." I explained to her that it's alright to wait on the LORD and that waiting on the LORD is a very divine and very heavenly thing to do; however, I then asked, "While you're waiting, what are you doing?" She seemed a little surprised by this question, as if she had never really considered such a question before. Such a question is designed to cause thought and action. You see, while you're waiting on GOD, there's an assignment to still enjoy the abundant life of the Kingdom of Heaven. While we're waiting, there's still a great, big world in existence all around us just waiting to be explored and enjoyed. This simple shift of perspective makes all the difference in the world, especially when viewing love and relationships and having the intention within our minds to begin the search for real and lasting love. Today, I want to encourage you to begin to view even the search in a much, much different way. Stop allowing yourself to be overwhelmed by the "work" of the search and begin to view the search as an adventure in which you simply begin to enjoy your life. This radical, yet simple shift of perspective will not only cause you to raise your own creative, attractive power and begin to draw into your life many more connections for relationship but it will also cause you to develop an even greater sense of confidence and optimism.

CHAPTER FIVE

In Chapter five of my book, entitled "Saying Goodbye," I tackle the painful and, at times, often random occurrence of breakups. As painful as a breakup is, every breakup is the beginning of a brand new chapter. As you read the chapter, you've realized that breakups, though painful, actually are quite divine and that, yes, even in the midst of pain and uncertainty, GOD is a part of the writing of your love story. Although in the painful and overwhelming emotions which surround the moment of a breakup and the ending of relationships it can seem like the end of the world, there is still hope, as long as we don't lose sight of our intended goal and our expected end. When a breakup occurs, one of both individuals find themselves reeling with a variety of emotions and a seemingly unexpected sense of uncertainty which always accompanies the unknown. However, in the moments of pain, if you can allow yourself to see the process of endings as merely a part of the beautiful cycle of new beginnings, not only will you prosper and flourish in your continued pursuit of love but you will also, in turn, keep your attractive power full and strong.

Far too often, when facing the pain of a breakup, it can feel like a literal death in the family. In many ways it is – the feelings and emotions of loss are often identical to the loss of a dear loved one or family member through death. A breakup is an ending. It's the severing of the bond, relationally speaking, and the beginning of a period of unexpected transition. Transitions, let's face it, are rarely easy and they always, always bring with them a sense of the unexpected. However, even in the midst of uncertain and overwhelming emotions, it actually is possible to keep your energy levels high and to maintain a sense of heavenly optimism. Remember, we are not as those who have no hope. In the chapter I shared the story of a real-life client of mine – a mother who after years of marriage found herself facing the unexpected loss of her marriage. In her testimony, she described how at the time of the initial breakup there were such mixed and uncertain, confusing feelings. These feelings of uncertainty and questioning are common to all breakups, regardless of the reason, I've found. As we move from the place of grieving to the place of acceptance, the journey is often clouded with many varying, seemingly contradictory emotions. If we were to think of a breakup in much the same way we would of the loss or death of a loved one, it isn't difficult to see exactly why the feelings of uncertainty can seem so very overwhelming and so, so very dark.

You're familiar; I'm sure, with the process of coping with loss commonly defined as the "7 stages of grief." Well, did you know that the same stages are involved in literally each and every breakup and ending of a romantic relationship? In a brilliantly written article for *Psychology Today*, entitled "The 7 Stages of Grieving a Breakup," Dr. Suzanne Lachmann writes, "The drive to know is consuming and can come at the expense of rational thoughts and behaviors. You must understand why this happened, maybe beyond anyone's ability to explain it. You fixate on things your ex said at various times that you see as contradicting the breakup, and you hold onto them now as if they are gospel. Yet somewhere within, you have moments of clarity, too. You likely swing back and forth between foggy disbelief, the daily, moment by moment rediscovery of the magnitude of your loss, and flashes of painful clarity that of course it's over. The pain, disorganization, and confusion can become all you think about, or talk about. But initially, you remain driven to understand what happened, at any cost. The desperation to make sense of something so jarring compels you to debate friends, family, coworkers, even strangers, about why the relationship ended, while you justify to them the reasons it shouldn't have, as if convincing them it is equal to convincing your ex." In other words, in every breakup, there's the overwhelming feeling of the need to analyze and to find answers. "Why did this happen?" "What did I do?" "What could I have done differently?" Well, regardless of the answers to those questions, know that the reason was never that you weren't good enough or were somehow undeserving of love.

Think of those moments in your life when a breakup occurred or when a close connection ended, whether platonic or romantic. As you think back, perhaps even now, you find yourself facing a series of emotions that just seem to come flooding back again, as the wounds of the past are reopened and reexamined. It's totally and completely natural. Part of why I chose to and felt led to include the chapter "Saying Goodbye" in the book is because I want you to begin to examine and to view even breakups in a very different way, from a much more spiritual and heavenly perspective. Although it isn't easy and although there really is no magical formula that can help to alleviate the pain of loss, the truth is that there are techniques which can help to bring forth the feeling of resolution and acceptance. Sometimes, in truth, goodbyes are necessary, and as much as you love the other person, it's alright to love yourself also. Self-love and self-acceptance is needed in all of our relationships in life – especially romantic ones and those with heightened, emotional intensity.

In the same article described above, by Dr. Lachmann, she also mentions the feeling of acceptance that, although difficult to navigate, will ultimately come after a breakup happens. She writes of Stage 7, titled "Redirected Hope," "You were leveled by the breakup and have had difficulty letting go, in part because it shattered your relationship with hope. As acceptance deepens, moving forward requires redirecting your feelings of hope—from the belief that you can singlehandedly save a failing relationship to the possibility that you just might be okay without your ex. It's jarring when forced to redirect your hope from the known entity of the relationship into the abyss of the unknown. But this is an opportunity to redirect the life force of hope. Regardless, hope is somewhere in your reserves and you will access it again as you continue to allow some meaningful distance between you and your ex. The stages of grief that follow any trauma, breakups included, can happen over the course of minutes or even seconds, across days, months, or years, and then switch around without warning, leaving you feeling without foundation, especially in the beginning. You feel alien to yourself or cut off from the world. However, like any emotional amputation, continuing on in life means learning to live without that part of yourself, and finding ways to compensate for its loss. Furthermore, recognize that there is a method, and a structure of sorts to this chaotic grieving process. Knowing that you are not alone can help you ride it out. Your grieving is part of the human condition—without it, we would not be wired the way we are to handle the many pains and losses that occur in our lives. As the grieving process progresses you will begin to see your way through to a point at which you can let go in a more proactive and self-protective way—a way that you may eventually come to understand as a new beginning."

I couldn't agree more. With all moments of transition – especially breakups – it's vitally important that you not lose hope. It is the sense of hopelessness that stifles the creative, attractive power of the universe. Hopelessness says, "I suppose I deserved it." Hopelessness says, "I can never have good things." Hopelessness says, "I suppose it will always end up this way." However, hope and the eyes of the Holy Spirit say, even in the midst of the most excruciating and overwhelming pain, "Even this is for my good." Hope says, "In spite of even this setback, good things are in store for my life and I am determined to continue to write my love story."

CHAPTER SIX

Chapter six of *Attracting Your Godly Spouse* is a chapter entitled "Moving Forward." I chose to include this chapter in the book because so very often, after a breakup, when facing the emotions of uncertainty that so often naturally arise in the period of transition, there are so many questions about how to actually begin the search again. In other words, "How do I begin the search again, even after unexpected moments and apparent setbacks?" In reading this chapter, you'll find that the emphasis is on forward motion and the ability to keep moving, in spite of the desire to stay still and become paralyzed. So often, when speaking to my in-person clients that I coach and counsel prophetically, I'm so often asked about this stage in the process of finding true love the most. "Jeremy, what happens when the connections don't seem to be working the way I want?" "What do I do when it seems like none of the new relationships are what I want or expected them to be?" I'm literally asked these questions on a daily basis when speaking prophetically into the lives of those who, like you, are searching for the romance of their dreams. My advice to them, as well as to you, is no matter what, "Keep moving forward!"

In the chapter I shared a very real account of two very dear friends of mine who, after experiencing unexpected setbacks in mutual breakups, found themselves not really knowing what to do to move forward. There was a state of paralysis for both. These two individuals, who lived within the same apartment complex, were seemingly complete polar opposites. On the surface level, they had very little in common – at last to the natural eye. However they both had a shared experience of pain and heartbreak and loss after unexpected breakups. This commonality forged a friendship, in the most unexpected and most unlikely of ways. Being that the two individuals were neighbors, they both began the friendship based on the fact that they had, pretty much, gone through the same thing. I emphasize this illustration in the chapter to say that even in the most unlikely of situations and circumstances, it's vitally, vitally important to be open to relationships in all their unique, different, and varying forms. Something truly powerful happens the moment that we begin to stop "searching" for love and simply begin to enjoy the people around us. Our energy levels are raised and our confidence is boosted. If you want to truly begin to attract into your life the romance and the passion you've been dreaming of, the first thing you're going to have to do is become much more open to honoring even the platonic friendships in your life. In other words, although not everyone will be a match or suitable candidate for you as far as romance is concerned, literally everyone in your life has a unique story to share, and it's important that you begin to see it if you're ever going to truly begin to master your own creative, attractive power.

In your life, are you able to say that you've surrounded yourself with people who are like-minded and who have a few of the same shared experiences? We'll touch on the importance of platonic relationships a little later on, but, as far as the people in your life, do you have a few truly close friends and confidants to enjoy life with? These connections are vitally important. Although these connections aren't forged from the desire to become romantically involved, these connections serve to provide for us a support system as we go about life. Simply put, you need friends. No one is an island, as the old saying goes. For those who truly know me personally, they know that, to me, there is absolutely nothing more important that friendship. There's a difference, you see, between being surrounded by people of all sorts and having many, many acquaintances and actually having true friends. I'm a truly blessed man to have such dear friends and loved ones in my life – people who love me and know me. Your inner circle matters greatly, especially if you are going to ever raise your energy to the level required for mastering your creative, attractive power. Friendships are often forged in the most uncanny, unusual, remarkable, and, at times, most unlikely of ways. You don't have to have the exact same shared experiences serve as the basis of a friendship; all that is required is an understanding and an acceptance. In other words, friendship relationships say, "Although you and I don't share the exact same story, I honor you and I honor your story." Friendship connections serve to say, "Thank you for allowing me to be a part of the story of your life. Thank you for trusting me."

I included this chapter for an even more important, all-powerful reason, however, and that is to highlight the powerful rise in creative energy we begin to exude and send out into the universe when, after unexpected moments and setbacks, we decide to still form bonds of relationship with people – even when they aren't of a romantic nature. Picture this. So often we view finding a romantic relationship as the sort of catch-all, end-all of the journey of life. We so often act like that's all that there is, when the reality is that romantic relationships are truly just one form of many, many different types of relationships. I promise you, my friend, you're going to be surprised when you begin to stop looking at every person as a candidate or as an option for romance and simply begin to see people as unique individuals with stories to share. In other words, my friend, start valuing all of your relationships – not just your romantic interests. When you begin to do this, you'll soon see that the energy of love and acceptance you are beginning to exude will draw into your life even more compatible options and candidates for romance.

Everything begins within the mind. Whether you know it or not, part of the reason you have yet to actually find the lasting relationship you've been dreaming of is because, well, you're looking too hard. I know that probably seems like a contradictory statement and right now you must be thinking, "Jeremy, what does that even mean?" Well, allow me to explain. Many times we enter into the search for romantic relationships purely out of fear – the fear of being alone. Again, please keep in mind that it's our intention which truly matters. If you're constantly waking each day set solely on finding a romantic partner, you'll be unsuccessful, because the universe is taking notice of your true intention. Your true intention, as it were, is not actually a desire to find love but is, rather, a fear-based desire to not be alone. Notice the difference? However, when you begin to enjoy your life, enjoy your day, and truly begin to honor all of the many different and unique relationships in your life – even the platonic ones – then you are actually signaling to the universe and to all of Heaven and earth that, yes, you are content in your own life and are pleased with the life you have. In other words, quite simply put, in order to attract more, first be grateful for what you already have.

CHAPTER SEVEN

Chapter seven of *Attracting your Godly Spouse* is a chapter entitled "Becoming More Attractive" and, in complete honesty, it was one of my favorite chapters to write because it details the importance of getting a makeover – a makeover the of the mind, that is. Although in previous chapters I touched briefly upon the importance of being able to recognize the energy behind relationship connections, in chapter seven I finally revealed the complete and brutally honest truth about why you have yet to meet the person of your dreams. The truth, though, is a very inconvenient truth and the emotions associated with accepting the truth may seem a little uncomfortable at first. The reason you have yet to attract the person of your dreams and desires actually isn't the fault of the other people out there and it isn't the fault of the universe or because GOD is somehow neglecting your desires and your dreams regarding finding lasting love. No, the reason, my friend, is your very own self. In truth, you've been the only person holding yourself back.

Personal responsibility is the chief bedrock of the universal Law of Attraction, and the process by which we begin to take personal responsibility – the process of taking a long, hard look in the mirror – is often times a very painful one. It's a bitter pill. It's an inconvenient truth. It's necessary, though. One of the main reasons I felt inspired to include the chapter in the book is because I want you to know just how vitally important it is to begin taking personal responsibility for your own life and to, even more so, take responsibility for your own thoughts and your own energy. Am I saying that everything that happened was your fault? Absolutely not. The abuse? The last breakup? The heartbreak? No, chances are much of it was in no way your fault. It was all unfair and you in no way deserved it. However, now that it's done, you and you alone are responsible for how you will choose to move forward. Only you, now, can make the decision to change and to heal and to raise your vibrational energy.

When I speak of the importance of a getting a makeover, I'm in no way referring to a makeover of the physical image that you see staring back at you as you look into the mirror each morning. No, I'm referring, instead, to the much-needed makeover of the mind. If you're ever going to truly begin to master your own thoughts and create your life and draw into your life the people and the experiences that you truly want and desire, you're going to have to, first, change your mind. You're going to have to begin to incorporate into the story of your life all of your experiences, rather than fragmenting over the past and hiding from the experiences of your life. You know as well as I do that we overcome by the power of our testimonies. This overcoming, though, is much more than a prayer or some miracle of divine healing – it is the practical approach to a new way of living and, furthermore, a new, practical approach to the way you view the story of your own life and your own history. You've hidden behind the past for far, far too long, and I love you enough to tell you that truth. The entire time you're waiting and hiding, you aren't getting any younger and time, in this world, is quickly passing you by. Aren't you truly ready to begin to live again? Aren't you ready, finally, to begin to experience the life of your dreams, without the crippling and debilitating agony of fear and insecurity? In order to do this, you're going to have to not only begin to accept the story of your life; you're going to have to, even more importantly, own the story of your life. We accomplish this by recognizing that regardless of the events of the past and regardless of the reasons, today is a brand new day and I am still writing the story of my life. GOD is not finished with you yet, and, truly, all things are working together for your good.

When I speak of becoming more attractive and giving yourself a makeover of the mind, I'm speaking primarily of learning to raise your energy and become more conscientious of what you are sending out to the universe with your thoughts.

When the universe sees you, does it see a victim or does it see an overcomer? Only you can decide that. Yes, Jesus has redeemed the past; however you and only you can integrate your past into the totality of your life so that you can become a complete and whole person. My friend, I say with all love and with all grace, there isn't a prayer meeting, there isn't a revival service, there isn't a prophetic word, and there isn't an angel in Heaven capable of doing for you what you will begin to do for yourself the moment you begin to fully take responsibility for your own life, your own energy, and your own thoughts. The choice, though, is yours and yours alone.

In my best-selling book *Creating with Your Thoughts* I shared how, metaphysically speaking, the universe and all of Heaven and earth are simply waiting to give us what we truly want and desire. The reason, though, that you've been receiving so much of what you don't want is, in part, because you've yet to fully embrace yourself in order to know what it is that you do want and, secondly, you've made excuse after excuse to keep from moving forward and owning your past experiences. It's time to change that, my friend. It's time to begin to truly recognize that you and you alone are responsible for the energy you are projecting into the universe with your thoughts. The universe is giving you more of what you are thinking. This, my friend, is why is can often times be painful to accept personal responsibility.

Metaphysically speaking, there is a very real and literal power behind our thoughts – a very real field of energy radiating from us at all times. With each thought, there are new neural pathways being formed within the brain and, due to the science and biochemistry of neural plasticity, you and I are constantly, constantly molding and reshaping our brains each and every day, based entirely upon the most predominant thoughts we choose to dwell upon. There's energy in the body – a very real energy of creation – and it stems from the world of inner thought. The study of metaphysics is, in simple terms the study of that which is "beyond" or "behind" the physical world. In a sense, it's the philosophical and even theological and ontological study of all that is. When you awaken to a new day and experience the world around you, you are seeing the world through conditioned perception and, as a result, are either judging your life as "good" or "bad" – as "satisfying" or as "unsatisfying." The moment you begin to see and truly recognize that the life you experience today is the result of the thoughts of yesterday you will truly begin to harness the all-powerful force of the inner Kingdom of Heaven within – the power of the Mind of Christ which is continuously creating through the Law of Attraction.

I also included this chapter, though to be a source of encouragement and to remind you that just as possible as it is to create the life you do not want, it is absolutely possible to also recreate life and to create the life you do want, based entirely upon your thoughts. There is still hope for you, my friend. There is still an opportunity for you to begin to change your mind and, by so doing, change your life and change the relationships you are attracting. For far too long you've viewed love and relationships as merely some game of chance, saying to yourself, "Well, if it happens it happens and if it doesn't it doesn't." This thinking, my friend, is a lie and is the antithesis of how the Kingdom of Heaven truly operates. Today, it's time to begin to reclaim your energy and this is accomplished by taking full ownership of your own creative power, recognizing yourself as a co-creator with GOD. I promise you that when you begin to take full ownership of your life and of your own energy, you will begin to attract into your life more of what you do want and far, far less of what you don't want. This applies especially to relationships.

CHAPTER EIGHT

In "The Beauty of Difference," chapter eight of my book *Attracting Your Godly Spouse*, I share a few principles that I believe to be beneficial when viewing all of our relationships we encounter throughout our lives – principles which help us to recognize the beauty of individuality. There truly is beauty in individuality and in uniqueness, if you think about it. Not everyone is like you, and that's a great thing. Individuality and uniqueness serve as reminders to us of just how great, vast, and filled with color all of Creation truly is. When the Creator, in the very beginning, formed the worlds and gave mankind dominion over Creation, He gave humanity unlimited access to a world filled with many wonderful and different sights and sounds and unique experiences. I often joke, "Did Adam and Eve have the same taste in foods or enjoy the same bands?" Although I say that jokingly, however, I believe the questions do serve to paint a picture of the importance of individuality.

If you're going to truly begin to harness your own creative attractive power and begin to rev up your magnetic energy, so to speak, you're going to have to also begin to recognize the brilliant and important beauty of difference. You're going to have to recognize that not everyone will have the same likes, the same interests, and the same tastes as you and, just as your characteristics make you wholly and completely who you are, others have their same traits, mannerisms, personal preferences, and tastes as well, and these many, many differences exist for a reason. I promise you that although it may not always seem like it, differences don't exist simply to rub you the wrong way or just for the purpose of challenging you. The beauty of difference is actually much, much more than that. Differences are in existence in Creation to give us a much better and even broader perspective of the heart and the mind of the Godhead. Differences remind us that Creation is a reflection of the personality of GOD and a view of what life in the Kingdom of Heaven is truly like.

Instead of viewing difference and contrast as liabilities in relationships – something to be avoided – begin to view the beauty of difference as an asset. All throughout the chapter, I included a few illustrations and true, real-life examples of how so very often we unfortunately have the misunderstanding successful relationships are only those relationships with those individuals who mirror us identically. This simply is not the case, my friend. In truth, to be completely honest, can you imagine how boring the world would be if everyone was identical to us? Now I'm not seeking to suggest that you aren't wonderful the way you are and that your interests and tastes aren't interesting. I'm simply saying that not everyone is like you and not everyone has had the exact same experiences to craft their worldview the same. You and I and all others are, to some degree, products of the filters we apply. Rather than viewing success as finding a person who believes exactly what you believe, likes what you like, enjoys what you enjoy, and shares your passions identically, why not begin to view success as finding a partner who is confident to be himself or herself while, all the while, being free enough to encourage you to be yourself?

So often I hear successful seemingly successful relationships defined in this way: "We're just alike! We can even finish each other's sentences!" I usually think to myself, "So, what? Big deal." When the glitz and the glamor of the honeymoon phase of the relationship ends, what's next? Where's the substance? You don't need someone to mirror or "parrot" you; you need someone to truly compliment you, and the art of complimenting is based in learning to recognize the beauty and the divine significance of difference – realizing full well that differences exist for a reason. According to the international data base of the Census Bureau, as of September 2018, the world population reached 7 billion people and will reach 8 billion individuals by the year 2025. Now, tell me again why you can't seem to find someone? These figures are astounding, as the number of unique individuals inhabiting this planet continues to climb and to grow. Not all of them share your tastes, your likes, or even your personality, and the truth of the matter is that the many, many differences exist by divine design.

It's time that you begin to view success in a much different way when thinking in terms of compatibility. Rather than viewing your search for true and lasting love as simply a sort of "Match Game," why not begin to view it in a more expansive way? If you view relationships as simply the search for someone to mirror you identically, I promise you, according to these staggering statistics, the numbers just aren't on your side. Stop looking at your search for love as simply a job in which you have to find someone to mirror you identically – that's far, far too overwhelming! Instead, begin to view the search for love in a much more spiritual way, through the lens of the Holy Spirit, knowing full well that difference exists for a very real and very divine reason. In the very beginning, when the love story was first enacted, the Creator didn't create clones. He created the beauty of a very real and very big world, with lots and lots of options. I assure you, there were times when Adam and Eve couldn't agree on what to have for dinner. And, well, even when they finally did, well, you know how *that* story goes.

CHAPTER NINE

Chapter Nine of the book is entitled "Be the One," and to be quite honest it was a very difficult chapter to write. It was difficult not because I was unsure of or uncertain of the truth to share, but, much like within the chapter entitled "Becoming More Attractive," the truth can, at times, be a very bitter pill to swallow. In Chapter Nine of *Attracting Your Godly Spouse*, I felt led to stress the importance of personal responsibility, again, but do so in an even more transcendent way by explaining further just how the Law of Attraction truly works in any and all of our relationship connections. Remembering that everything is based purely upon our own thoughts and our own intentions, it can often times be difficult to keep perspective of the importance of self-awareness. Self-awareness, much like confidence, in vital, especially when considering that we ourselves are the ones who are truly writing our love stories we enjoy.

In the chapter, I shared a very real account of a real-life client who several years ago had come to me for a prophetic reading. When approaching me, she wanted to inquire of the LORD what the Holy Spirit was saying about her love life. "Jeremy, when will I meet the person of my dreams?" She explained that the person of her dreams was a single, healthy, athletic, successful business owner who managed his own company, and she, in her own words, refused to settle for anything less than that. Although I admired her faith, as I listened intently to her, I couldn't help but feel a very real pushback from the Holy Spirit as she spoke. As I shared within the chapter, she explained to me how she had just dropped out of college and had just recently quit her part-time job and how, typically, most of her days were filled with binge-watching reality television and eating candy and drinking soda. If you know me then you know full well that I have a heart for people. I love people and never want to see anyone hurt or made to feel pain. However, those who truly know me also know that I love people enough to always be completely honest with them. As much as it truly, truly pained me to say it to her, the Word of the Lord to her was that she would not find this man of her dreams if she were to continue in her current mindset, in her current lifestyle. When she asked when she would meet him, I responded, simply, "You won't." In an instant I saw the pain of shock and bewilderment upon her face. I meant it with all my heart.

Now, let me say that there are no hopeless situations. Thankfully, you and I have the power to recreate the lives we now find ourselves living and, thankfully, if there's something that we would like to change, GOD has given us the power to create and to enact change. There was hope, even for her. The reason for the blockage and the overwhelming hindrance though is based entirely upon the heavenly principle of the universal Law of Attraction. In order to begin to get what you want, you must first begin to become what you want. In other words, you can't expect the universe or, for that matter, Heaven to give to you something that you aren't even attempting to do for yourself. It just doesn't work that way. The universe just doesn't work that way. We're given more of just what we're producing. If you're producing very little then you probably shouldn't expect much more, in all honesty. I say this because I love you.

For centuries, religion has promoted the erroneous lie that says, "GOD loves us so much He gives us everything we want." It simply isn't true. The more correct truth says, "GOD loves us so much that He invested within us the power to attract into our lives the things we want." See the difference? The difference lies in the role of personal responsibility. The Law of Attraction requires partnership. At all hours of the day and night, the universe and all of Heaven is giving us more and more of exactly what we are sending out through our actions, thoughts, and intention. What we sow, we will reap; there is no escaping it. In order to get what you truly want, action will be required on your part. In other words, suffice it to say, wanting without action is nothing more than just wishful thinking and daydreaming. Intention demands movement. If you're truly wanting to attract into your life the love and relationship of your dreams and desires then you no longer have the luxury of sitting idly by on the sidelines of life, waiting and hoping that something will change or that by some act of fate and by divine intervention GOD will miraculously drop into your lap the person of your dreams. If you want to attract the person you desire, then, I would ask, "What are you doing to become more attractive?" While you're waiting, what exactly are you doing? If you want a successful spouse, then begin to create success in our own life. If you want an athletic, fit spouse, then you can't sit on the couch eating Doritos all day and expect to meet him. It just doesn't work that way, my friend, and to think that a prayer will make it happen when you aren't placing yourself into alignment with your intention is just complete and utter nonsense. The Kingdom of Heaven operates by the heavenly and divine power of the universal Law of Attraction and the Law of

Attraction demands partnership and willing and active participation in the creation and attraction process.

Now, although I in no way expect you to earn or complete your degree within the next 90 days or, for that matter, even make your first million dollars through your own successful startup, what I am asking, my friend, is that you begin to place yourself into a position of better alignment with what and even who you profess to want. You see, you may say with your lips and may even desire with your heart to attract the person of your dreams and desires; however, your choices and your actions are revealing to the universe your true intention. When you sit idly by and wait, your intention is that you are content with the way things are. As a result, you receive even more of the exact same life you've chosen to settle for. The good thing, though, is that there is hope. Today is your NOW moment, and quite literally everything can begin to change the moment you determine within your heart and mind to become more strategically positioned and aligned with your desire. It's time to get up, get out, and get moving. It's time to begin to invest in yourself and actually signal to the universe and to all of Heaven that you care enough about your desires to begin to move toward your intended goal.

Within your own life, if you were to be completely honest, are there areas in which you've found yourself simply giving up or quitting? If so, then why? Are there dreams that you walked away from because of a feeling of hopelessness? Have there been times in which it's felt as though you've completely just stopped trying? If so, then I want to encourage you to begin to pick up your dreams again. I want you to pick up your feet and begin to move. Begin to invest in yourself and begin to better yourself once again. Take the class. Enjoy the trip. Begin the new exercise regimen you've been talking about. Start the new diet. Research ways to finally start the business you've been dreaming of. My point is quite simply, really. Do something. Do anything to begin to move again. But do not; under any circumstance continue to do the same thing you've been doing and expect for GOD to give you the person of your dreams. I assure you, He will absolutely not.

CHAPTER TEN

"Expectancy" is the title to the tenth chapter of *Attracting Your Godly Spouse*, and in many ways it is a much needed reality check for those searching for true and lasting love. For far too long, we've been conditioned and programmed to have such unrealistic views and expectations of what successful relationships look like, is it any wonder we so often set ourselves up for failure? Is it truly any wonder, really, that so many relationships end in failure before ever truly beginning to blossom, when we've looked to popular movies, romance novels, and fairy tales to provide to us the definition of "love?" I'm not suggesting in any way that you lower your standard or, in some way, begin to lessen the dream. What I am saying, though, is that in your search for love, it's important to be realistic and to have a healthy dose of pragmatism.

When *Fifty Shades of Grey*, the blockbuster film based upon the novel by E. L. James, was released, it earned more than half a billion dollars at the box office - $570,998,101 to be exact. This erotic thriller was followed by two additional films, each based upon the books within the series. As important as passion, chemistry, and, yes, even sex are to the human experience, is it really any wonder we so often find ourselves feeling a sense of disappointment or a lack of chemistry when our significant other or future partner comes along missing a private jet and a billion dollar bank account? Is it any wonder why you've sometimes found yourself disappointed in your own search for love when you just can't seem to reenact the scene at the end of *Breakfast at Tiffany's*? Can you really blame yourself for feeling let down when, for years growing up, you were told that one day a white knight in shiny armor will come to your rescue and solve literally all of your problems and sweep you off your feet? Of course not. The irrational conditioning of society to view "The One" in such outrageous ways is in no way your fault. However, the management of your own expectation is completely, completely your own personal responsibility.

Although success can and should always be defined as the attaining of an expected outcome or expected end result, I want to ask you, today, just exactly what do you expect your ideal relationship to look like? What do you expect him to be like? How do you expect her to be? Truly? I hate to be the bearer of bad news, but if you're thinking that someone will come along with the ability to be a savior and rescue you from the life you've created for yourself, you're going to be sorely disappointed and sorely mistaken. Rather than set yourself up for eminent heartbreak and the failure of a relationship, why not begin to manage your expectations in a much more practical, spiritually-minded way and begin to recognize that we are, at the end of the day, all real people, living real lives, in a very, very real world. The sooner you begin to recognize this, the better you'll be for it, I assure you. According to the American Psychological Association, the divorce rate within the United States is currently

50%, with the divorce rate for subsequent marriages being even higher. Although I in no way seek to suggest that your marriage will fall into this category, I cannot help but ask, of all of those marriages which ended in divorce, how many of them do you think ended simply because the reality of relationship failed in comparison to the unrealistic and unhealthy expectations that were placed upon those marriages going in? I'm sure that, like you, there were those who entered the marriage relationship thinking of the dreams and the fairy tale to be shared. Only, for most, those dreams were dashed the moment the rubber met the road, as they say, and the reality of real life began to quickly sink in. Whatever the reason, though, I want to encourage you today by reminding you that you don't have to become just another statistic. You don't have to settle for the status quo of what comes from unrealistic expectations unsuccessfully and unrealistically managed. Rather than looking for someone to "complete you," like the star in some Hollywood film, why not, instead, choose to view yourself as already complete and, in turn, begin to view success in a loving relationship as two complete, whole people learning to do life together and sharing in the adventure of experience.

CHAPTER ELEVEN

Chapter Eleven of *Attracting Your Godly Spouse* is a chapter entitled "Unclaimed Baggage," and it's, in many ways, a title that illustrates the importance of recognizing the wounds of the past while at the same time learning to be very selective and very careful of who we allow into our lives. Although there's great, great beauty in difference, the fact is that sometimes we have to become much more selective of whom we allow into our lives to begin with. Often, before we ever even truly realize it, we can find ourselves drained and left weakened by the negativities of others, all because we never took the time to stay vigilant in protecting ourselves, our boundaries, and our own interests. Relationships are all about the art of learning to relate; however, there are very real times in which boundaries must be drawn for our own safety and our own peace of mind. These boundaries are important because they not only protect us and help us to reclaim our own sense of self, but they also signal to the universe and to others that we value ourselves enough to sometimes walk away from those things which are not for our greatest and highest good.

I also felt led to include this chapter for another, perhaps even more important reason, though, which is to illustrate that so often there are things within our lives – unhealed wounds, past scars, and past traumas, that we simply have just forgotten about that are continuing to affect us on a subconscious level. We all have baggage in some way or another. We all have those moments from the past that have in some way helped to shape us and to form the basis of the story of our lives – the face – that we present to the outside world around us. Often, though, the reason that we've forgotten about these things is not simply a lack of memory but rather a sense of repression and a desire to hide. This sense of hiding changes both our own level of energy and our intention, and the universe takes notice, even when we consciously don't. Healing is important and healing is very real. The greatest healing, though, is quite often the healing from our own pasts that we must allow ourselves.

As you've progressed through the book, *Attracting Your Godly Spouse*, you've felt a variety of emotions and have been forced to confront yourself in ways that probably found unexpected. The book is specifically designed to cause this self-reflection and introspection. I know that you were probably thinking when you purchased the book that there would be some divine, magical formula offered to you to help you magically draw someone into your life. Well, there is; however, the power of attraction that comes only when we incorporate into our own lives and into our own selves the self-awareness that the universe is demanding of us. The magic happens when we do the often uncomfortable work of getting in touch with ourselves and learning to discover who we truly are. My hope is that as you've progressed through the book you've taken time to also complete a section of my specially designed workbook which coincides with the book, as well. The workbook, *Attracting*

Your Godly Spouse: A Workbook in Attraction, is designed to serve as a rigorous intensive which will boost your own attractive and creative power even to a greater degree and cause you to harness your dreams and desires as you begin to implement and put into practice the teachings of this series in a very real and practical way in your day-to-day life. What I've found is that, in truth, there really is a certain kind of heavenly magic – the power of the Kingdom of Heaven within – which truly does begin to take full effect the moment we begin to look more deeply within to see who we truly are.

Often the wounds of the past manifest as shadows within our lives and as dark places which have yet to be fully integrated. As I've said and taught for years, healing is a sense total and complete wholeness. You cannot be completely and totally whole until you truly begin to fully own the story of your life and accept responsibility for your past. Until you do this, there will always be the weight of "unclaimed" baggage which will continue to follow you and weigh you down with unnecessary, added weight, keeping you from truly and fully enjoying the freedom of actually getting to know someone better and more intimately. What I've found through years of coaching and counseling is that for many, there are areas of the past that have yet to be fully embraced – fully owned. These pieces of "unclaimed" baggage are literally like ticking time bombs in relationships which can and will detonate at the most unlikely and most unexpected of times.

As you look to your own life, being as completely truthful and as transparent with yourself as possible, can you identity moments in relationships in which you haven't fully been able to be yourself and have lashed out in defensiveness without ever really knowing why? Have you, at times, surprised even yourself with your behavior in relationships or in your actions toward others without ever really knowing why you've felt so guarded as though there's something to hide? The reason is that you have unclaimed baggage, my friend. Old wounds and old traumas from the past that are continuing to follow you from relationship to relationship are only adding extra, added weight to you and are keeping you from fully being able to experience and enjoy new connections. The way in which we begin to heal from the past is to finally begin to make the decision to own the past, recognizing that, yes, it happened and that, yes, you're better for it because all things have worked together for your good.

Today, as you think of your own life and of the connections you make within your life, can you identify several key traits of guardedness or evasiveness which sometimes manifest within you as you attempt to meet new and interesting people? As you make your approach to the person with whom you feel a sense of attraction and chemistry, do you at times feel an inner, invisible barrier – an inner wall – within you keeping you from fully being yourself? If so, to be quite honest, the other person is probably noticing that guardedness and evasiveness you're exuding also. From initial encounters to first meetings to those first few moments of conversation with that new, special someone, without an ability to fully be present in the moment, things simply stall. That new, special someone wants to know you – the real you. Whether you choose to let them into your life is entirely, completely your decision and yours alone; however, never let the reason the relationship fails or doesn't progress ever be because you haven't been authentically and completely your true self.

CHAPTER TWELVE

In the chapter titled "Finally," the twelfth chapter of my book *Attracting Your Godly Spouse*, I discuss something that, in my humble opinion, is rarely ever talked about which is "What happens when you finally *do* meet that special someone?" What happens once the connection *is* made and the connection finally begins to progress into the relationship of your dreams and desire? So you've finally met the special someone who seems to be the answer to your prayers and the end result of years of searching. Now what? I included this chapter because, in my opinion, even after finally making the lasting connection the work continues and the journey of self-improvement remains ongoing. Just because you've finally met your own special someone, the need to integrate and self-actualize doesn't end; in fact, the work is truly just beginning, in all honesty.

So often I hear accounts of relationships ending after four or five or ten or even twenty years, in which one or both individuals simply quit trying and gave up and decided to walk away. Usually this decision to walk away is regretted by both individuals, more times than not. In the chapter I included an account of a person who walked away from a relationship once the feeling of chemistry ended, only to, soon after, begin to regret her decision and want him back. It's all too common, really, those times in which the moments of chemistry seemingly end and the honeymoon phase seems to fade and one or both individuals simply decide it's no longer worth it. Many times this feeling arises because one or both individuals simply failed to manage their expectations of the relationship in a healthy way. Other times it arises simply because we as individuals are always looking out for the new and the fun. But what happens when the relationship is no longer fun and exciting and when the initial newness that was so evidently there in the beginning begins to wear off?

What then? Well, my friend, that's when the work continues and is, in truth, needed more than ever.

Love is not a feeling; love is a decision. I hope that as you've progressed through the book you've come to that realization on your own, in some way. Like all decisions we make, we do possess the power to change our minds and to reassess. We do possess the power to make other decisions. However, regarding relationships and the connections we make throughout our lives – connections which deal with matters of the heart – I would urge caution when choosing to simply give up or quit or walk away. Know yourself well enough to know your true reasoning. Are you walking away simply because you're tired and want something new or are you walking away because you've just become too lazy to keep trying? Only you will be able to answer that question for yourself, should the time ever come. Should that time come, though, I hope and pray for your sake that you are at least honest enough with yourself to be genuine about your decision and fully own your decision. Because, if you aren't you will regret it, I promise you, and it will haunt you for years.

It's alright to walk away from a connection that is unsatisfying and it's alright to end a relationship which no longer honors you; however, never mistake your own laziness for the feeling of no longer being satisfied, because the two can, at times, look and feel quite identical, as I discussed within the chapter. Often, when coaching couples who have entered into a relationship or a marriage, I so often hear, "Jeremy, he just isn't the same person he was when we met" or "Jeremy, she just seemed to change and suddenly quit trying." More times than not, though, what I'm truly hearing as I read prophetically between the lines is, "Jeremy, the honest truth is that we're *both* too lazy to do the work." At the end of the day, that's it, really. In your life, as you look back at some of the relationships you've encountered and enjoyed within your life, perhaps there were times that you simply walked away because you just lost the desire to keep trying. Now, as you look back, it's alright to admit that. It's alright and it's healthy to admit that. Own it. Take ownership of the decision. But in taking ownership of the decision to walk away, be honest and genuine about your reasoning, or else you will be destined to repeat the same process in your next relationship.

Chapter Eleven, in all honesty, is a chapter which details the vast importance of learning to realize that all of our relationships in life require a certain amount of effort and a certain amount of work to be maintained. They require communication and vulnerability. The require dedication. Above all else, they require a certain amount of understanding. These aspects of the work will always be required, long, long after the first initial meeting and long after the vows are exchanged. I shared this chapter with you because I want you to recognize, now, that the love you say you truly want will be a love worth working to keep. The love you say you want will be a love that will require moments of maintenance and moments of upkeep. Recognizing that, now, before ever making the decision to walk away when the honeymoon period ends will be one of the greatest lessons you will ever learn. Love is worth finding. Love is also worth keeping.

A WORD FROM JEREMY

Throughout my life and career in ministry, I've had the opportunity to coach and to counsel individuals from all throughout the world regarding a variety of topics. I've been so blessed to have ministered prophetically to heads of business as well as heads of state. At the end of the day, though, from Prime Ministers to heads of Fortune 500 Companies to single mothers to the divorced father, we all have one thing in common: a desire to love and to be loved. Throughout my career and ministry, I've had the opportunity to write many books – more than thirty, actually, with many of them becoming international best-sellers. I'm truly blessed and so very thankful for the privilege and the opportunity you've given me to speak into your life all these years. But this book series is truly the first of its kind, I believe. Of all the questions I've been asked over the years, perhaps the one that arises the most is, "Jeremy, when will I find the love of my life?" I hear the question literally each and every day and have for more than twenty years.

I wrote *Attracting Your Godly Spouse* as an all-inclusive answer to that and presented the book in a way that would, hopefully, not only answer the question but would also share practical, powerful tips on how to not only attract a relationship but to attract the exact relationship you've been dreaming of. If you've followed my work for any amount of time then you know, prophetically speaking, it is the Law of Attraction which GOD established in the very beginning which serves as the basis of the creation and manifestation of each and every dream we have. In the very beginning, long, long ago in a garden paradise, when boy met girl for the first time, there was also enacted a Law of Creation and a Law of Attraction. The Law of Attraction is evident in literally all that we do, all that we seek, all that we encounter, and, yes, it's at work in literally all of our relationship connections – the platonic ones and especially the romantic ones.

I wrote the book and also the subsequent teaching series for you, my friend, to help you not only better understand that you truly do have the power to attract into your life the relationship of your dreams but that you have the power to attract into your life even the exact person of your dreams, if you do the work of learning to know yourself and to harness your own thoughts. This isn't some magical formula for finding true love, my friend; its's the simply truth of the Kingdom of GOD. I share this with you because I want you to know that, yes, it is possible to attract into your life the relationship and the romance that you've been desiring and that, yes, you have a divine right to want, to expect, and to receive real and lasting love in all its many, many forms. However as with all things, the responsibility rests solely on you. When you begin to do the work of knowing yourself, first, and looking within into your true self – into the inner Kingdom of Heaven which resides within you – you will be forced to answer a very important question: "What am I giving?" The answer to this question will directly determine what you are sending out into the universe based upon your thoughts, and, my friend, the universe and all of Heaven and earth will respond to the way in which you answer that question. What are you giving to the world around you? What are you giving to those you love and cherish? What are you giving in your relationships and in your friendships now? Long before ever entering into a true and lasting love affair, Heaven will demand that you take ownership of your life and take personal responsibility for what you are thinking even now, in your singleness. Once you begin to master your thoughts, you will be able to have anything and everything you desire – including the person of your dreams. I promise you this. In all things, I wish you love and much more of it.

Love,

Jeremy

ABOUT THE AUTHOR

Dr. Jeremy Lopez is Founder and President of Identity Network and Now Is Your Moment. Identity Network is one of the world's leading prophetic resource sites, offering books, teachings, and courses to a global audience. For more than thirty years, Dr. Lopez has been considered a pioneering voice within the field of the prophetic arts and his proven strategies for success coaching are now being implemented by various training institutes and faith groups throughout the world. Dr. Lopez is the author of more than thirty books, including his best-selling books The Universe is at Your Command and Creating With Your Thoughts. Throughout his career, he has spoken prophetically into the lives of heads of business as well as heads of state. He has ministered to Governor Bob Riley of the State of Alabama, Prime Minister Benjamin Netanyahu, and Shimon Peres. Dr. Lopez continues to be a highly-sought conference teacher and host, speaking on the topics of human potential, spirituality, and self-empowerment. Each year, Identity Network receives more than one millions requests from individuals throughout the world seeking his prophetic counsel and insight.

ADDITIONAL WORKS

Prophetic Transformation

The Universe is at Your Command: Vibrating the Creative Side of God

Creating With Your Thoughts

Crating Your Soul Map: Manifesting the Future You with a Vision Board

Creating Your Soul Map: A Visionary Workbook

Abandoned to Divine Destiny

The Law of Attraction: Universal Power of Spirit

And many, many more.

Made in the USA
Lexington, KY
22 December 2018